I WIN

WHAT ABOUT YOU?

MICHELA BARR

HAPPY FAMILY
—— Press ——

© 2023 Happy Family Press. All rights reserved.
I Win. ISBN: 978-1-7391860-3-6.

No part of this publication may be reproduced, distributed or transmitted in any form or by any means, including photocopying, recording or other electronic and mechanical methods, without prior permission in writing from the author and publisher, except for the use of a brief quotation in a book review or certain other non-commercial uses permitted by copyright law.

Email: info@happyfamilypress.com

Address for the correspondence:
Helvellyn Limited trading as "Happy Family Press",
71-75 Shelton Street, Covent Garden, London, WC2H 9JQ, UK

To discover more of our books, scan the QR code or visit the website www.happyfamilypress.com. Thanks!

"It's raining, it's raining inside.
Yet outside everything seems dry."

"Where am I? I can't see anything. I'm lost."

─── ◆ ◆ ◆ ───

IT WAS DARK, TERRIBLY DARK.

BUT WHEN YOU REACH THE BOTTOM,
THERE IS NOWHERE ELSE TO GO BUT UP.
THE GROUND GIVES YOU THE PUSH YOU NEED TO RISE.

JUST LIKE BEING UNDER WATER,
YOU FEEL SUFFOCATED.

EVERYTHING'S STILL DARK, BUT AT A CERTAIN POINT
YOU ARE ASCENDING, BREATHING, YOU ARE ALIVE.

FINALLY YOU SEE THE LIGHT.

─── ◆ ◆ ◆ ───

"How are you?"

"I'm tired."

"Where are you?"

"I don't know."

"Ok, don't worry, it happened to me too. Honestly, I think it happens to everyone.

Let me show you the way so you can join us...

...because you definitely didn't come this far to give up."

"I understand. But do you see those GAPS?"

"WHAT GAPS?"

"The ones between the bars. Your worries are too big. You need to reshape your life, your situation. That way, your problems will become smaller, and you'll be able to pass. You'll find a way out."

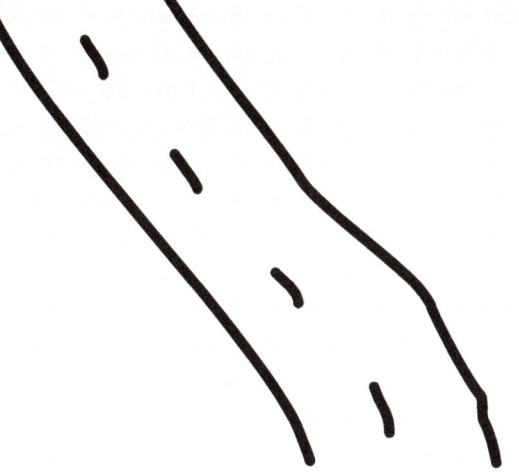

"FOR NOW, JUST CHOOSE A PATH. Sometimes you just have to wait a while, and many things will start to make sense. In the meantime, keep moving forward, one day at a time."

"You will never have everything under control. You can ONLY control your OWN actions. Start with those. Do your best and that's enough."

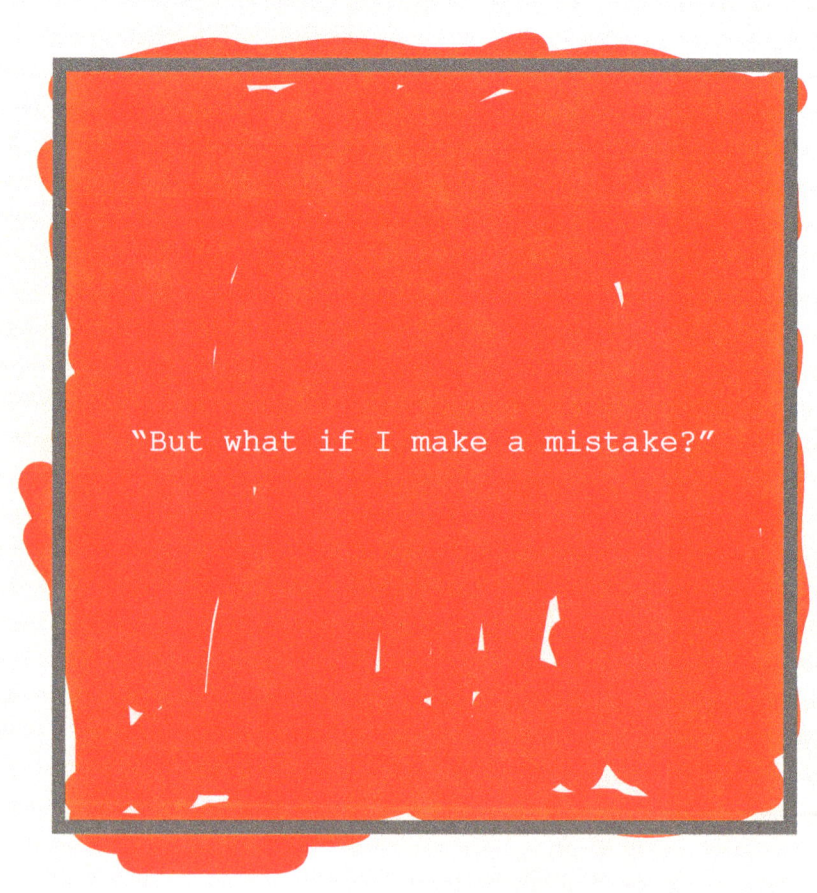

✓ Good! You are trying and learning!

"YOU'LL MAKE MISTAKES, YOU'LL STUMBLE AND THEN YOU'LL RISE AGAIN."

"Because that's life.

It tests you, and you go, Go, GO.

If you feel the need, take a rest.

But then get going again."

DON'T GIVE UP.

YOU WILL FALL.

BUT KEEP ON GOING.

"Don't let what happens around you, things you cannot change, change you.

Don't let those who treat you poorly to define your worth.

This is true freedom."

"Will I find HAPPINESS?"

"WHAT IS HAPPINESS FOR YOU?

Happiness is many things.

Sometimes being content is enough.

It's not always achievable.

But when you can, be content.

Things will never be perfect.

Embrace contentment whenever possible.

GRAB HOLD OF IT AND HOLD IT TIGHT. DEMAND IT."

"At times, it seems to me

that nothing has meaning.

I don't see the light.

I can't find the door."

"It's normal. You know,
sometimes, a walk helps.

Also, a relaxing shower,
clean sheets and
a good night's sleep.

Then tidy up.
Organize your room,
your home.

**Continue sorting through your thoughts,
little by little.**

Clear away the things
that don't matter.

Then focus on what
you can improve.

One thought at a time,
change what you can
and… slowly,
order will return."

"I DON'T HAVE THE STRENGTH. I don't feel motivated. I can't do it. I feel terribly exhausted."

"Why did you start?

Remember THIS.

And start again."

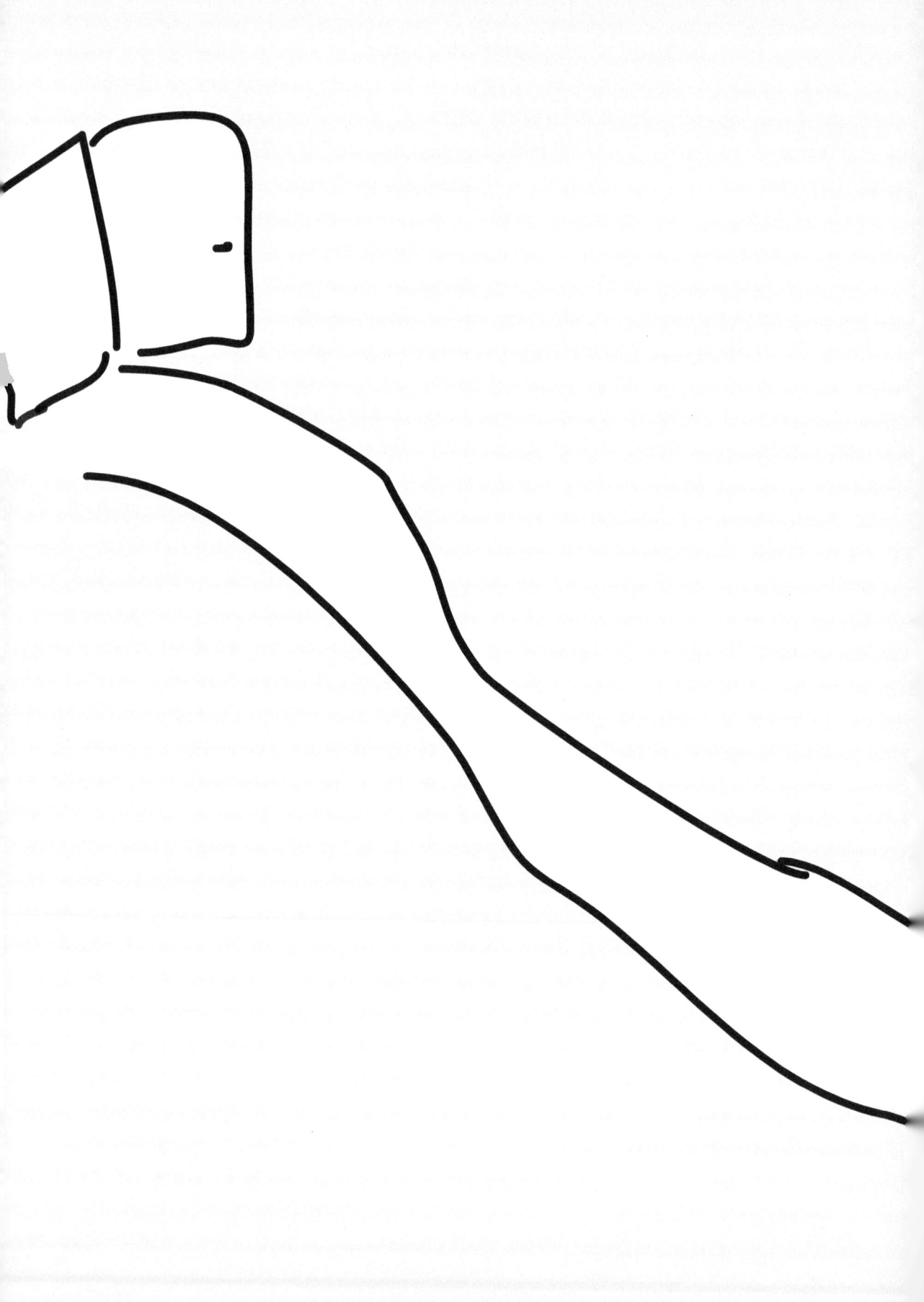

"The door will open, and the light will return."

I WANT TO WIN!

"But what does victory bring?"

"WHATEVER YOU WANT.

IT DEPENDS WHAT YOU ARE LOOKING FOR.

Some days it could even be stepping outside and facing the world out there."

"ON THE DARKEST DAYS, WHAT CAN I DO?"

"Helping others often helps us even more.
It makes us feel better.

Start there."

"Remember that you were born to win.
To give the best of yourself.

Treat yourself with the respect
and love you deserve.

And don't worry about the future,
there are many paths, you will find yours.

Sometimes it may seem like you've taken the
wrong one, but in reality, it's just part
of the journey that will lead you to your
destination."

I created this book for you, for me.

I wrote and illustrated it spontaneously, it's not supposed to be perfect, because nothing ever is.

It's supposed to be genuine. It's meant to be like a friend, a helpful support that fills a void and makes us feel better.

Because we don't give up.
WE WIN. ALWAYS REMEMBER THAT.

READ ME AND READ ME AGAIN.
In the morning, afternoon, evening, night.
Whenever you feel the need. Whenever you feel lost.

THEN GIVE ME AS A GIFT TO SOMEONE.
Everybody needs me as a reminder to never give up.

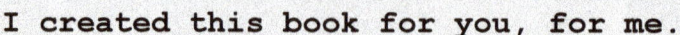

Let's move forward together. One step at a time, towards our victory. Whatever that may be.

MICHELA BARR

www.ingramcontent.com/pod-product-compliance
Lightning Source LLC
Chambersburg PA
CBHW042037100526
44587CB00030B/4470